NIGHT BEYOND BLACK

NIGHT BEYOND BLACK

LOIS PARKER EDSTROM

POEMS

MoonPathPress

Night Beyond Black

Poetry

ISBN 978-1-936657-21-6

Cover photo by Jim T. Johnson,
The Milky Way center from Anthony Lake, Oregon;
20-second exposure.

Author photo by Mel Edstrom

Book design by Tonya Namura
using Gentium Book Basic

MoonPath Press is dedicated to
publishing the finest poets of
the U.S. Pacific Northwest

MoonPath Press
PO Box 1808
Kingston, WA 98346

MoonPathPress@gmail.com

http://MoonPathPress.com

ACKNOWLEDGMENTS

Grateful acknowledgment is made to the editors of the following publications in which these poems first appeared.

Biopsy, Connecticut River Review, 2011

Café Terrace at Night, Hackney National Literary Award, Second Place, 2012

Cascade Suite, Dr. Zylpha Mapp Robinson International Poetry Award, First Honorable Mention, 2012. Published in Mobius Magazine, 2012

Choices We Make When We Are Too Young to Make Them, Poetry Society of New Hampshire, Second Place, 2012. Published in Poet's Touchstone, 2012

Cookie Bakers, Literary Mama, 2008. Appeared in chapbook, What Brings Us to Water, 2010

East of the Mountains, Adanna: Women and War, a Tribute to Adrienne Rich, 2013

Fifty Years Together, Adanna: A Collection of Contemporary Love Poems, 2012

Finding Our Way, Adanna: A Collection of Contemporary Love Poems, 2012

The Lesson of Plums, Adanna: Women and War, a Tribute to Adrienne Rich, 2013

Luncheon on the Grass, Adanna : A Journal for Women, about Women, 2011, Diane Lockward, Guest Editor

Tamarack, Floating Bridge Review, 2010

Tilt, The Westmoreland Award, Westmoreland Arts and Heritage Festival, March, 2014

Wellington Train Disaster, Finalist Mississippi Valley Writing Contest - Midwest Writing Center. Published in Off Channel, 2010

When Silence Was Enough, Appeared in chapbook, What Brings Us to Water, 2010

Where Poems Winter, Upper Delaware Writer's Collective, Second place, publication 2010

Yesterday's Light, Write Wing Publishing: Through a Distant Lens, 2013

Thanks to Teresa Wiley for her insightful comments, sharp wit, and enduring friendship and to Corey Cox who, with Teresa, provided a beautiful mountain retreat where many of these poems were written.

I'm indebted to Lorraine Healy who gave me a map and sent me on this journey and to Sheryl Clough and Diane Stone for sharing their love of poetry with me and for being unrelenting punctuation Ninjas.

My thanks and admiration to Lana Hechtman Ayers, Editor and Publisher at MoonPath Press, for her perceptive guidance and generous spirit.

To Evan Edstrom who is always there for me with hugs and the best technical support and to Emily Edstrom who advises me on all things beautiful – thank you. I am blessed to be surrounded by a creative family who inspire me daily. Thanks also to dear friends who fill my life with celebration and laughter; you know who you are.

for Evan & Emily

CONTENTS

Part Three

Part Four

CAFÉ TERRACE AT NIGHT

Oil on canvas, Vincent Van Gogh

Patrons cluster in sulfurous light
while he memorizes darkness, makes it bearable,
emerging, as he did, from gloomy Dutch interiors,
potato fields' dark furrows.

A night painting without black,
with nothing but beautiful blue and violet
and green, the strokes fall heavy,
at right angles to each other,

as if to make sense of that endless sky
where the stars wear coronas—
minor angels calling
to his upturned soul.

A cobbled road, like an uneven
life, leads away, bordered
by empty tables and chairs
just at the edge of light.

Remember the sunflowers' golden glow,
wheat ripening in a summer field,
heat that rises beneath troubled skies.
Nothing could stop those whorls of wild

blackbirds.

PART ONE

What makes the engine go?
Desire, desire, desire.
Stanley Kunitz

DAYBREAK

The morning air is all awash with angels.
Richard Wilbur

The morning air so still
the birds have stopped to listen,

the rustlings of night creatures
becalmed by dawn's measured light

and the moon which filled
Crockett Lake with the face of night

gives way to daybreak's stealth, a corrugated
shimmer across the surface of the lake.

Fresh from the drone of dreams
one scene lingers, oozes out of its hive.

My cloak, the exact magenta of sunrise,
streams behind me

as I run down curved stone steps
moving against the wind.

I can't say whether I'm fleeing
or advancing. In dreams, as in life,

one may never know. Poised
at the edge of morning's approaching

light, I see the kingfisher in stationary
position above the lake.

It prepares for the dive.

FLORA RUSTICA'S VALLEY

Fields of daffodils trumpet light
to a cerulean sky. No caution here,
my gaze arrested in the glare
of their bright glow; acres
and acres planted in precise rows
surround white farmhouses,
red barns, stop only at the upturn
of purple foothills.

Bail posted by the benevolence
of dusk, I turn toward home.
Along my path errant runaways
cluster in the middle of a spring-green
pasture, reach through the hedge
in the corner of a churchyard.
A single clump edges the parkway
as if bulbs were thrown
from a passing car.

Released from cultivated
expectations, these charmers
make the case for wildness.

OSTINATO

For Brent

Above the cove in a willow tree a bird sings,
hidden in spring's festivity—a three note
chromatic melody reproduced perfectly
again and again.

The notes, pure as the air through which they travel,
cannot be contained. They ride their exquisite waves
to the nautilus within my ear.

How we love repetition, an echo of sonar through
embryonic waters, counting on the comfort of response,
yet listening breathless for unexpected change.

Did birds first inspire music, or do we hear melodies
that float in the brine of our inner tides?

RAW LUCK

There was a time my life
    stretched out like an infinite sea,

no thought of a beginning or end,
    obstacles a dim range viewed from afar.

It may have been the animal body
    of youth, devoid of dreams or aspirations.

Was it good to live
    in those moments, those years

walking along the shore of choice
    without realizing how dreams

could fill the sail of sky?
    I may never know, yet somehow

I stepped lightly into my life
    realizing what I needed to be nourished

the way the sun, if you follow the seed,
    feeds the bird.

EROTICA IN UPTOWN

Port Townsend, Washington

Floured footprints lead us down a side street
to the door—*Pane d' Amore.*

Inside croissants curl against each other
like familiar bed partners.

Currant scones rest side by side,
foccacia nudges Swedish limpa,

ciabbata reclines near mounded rounds,
braided loaves, love-knots—steamy,

yeasty-breathed, and those perky baguettes
that flare like lust from a wicker basket.

I stare until it seems rude; twisted exhibitionists
stacked high against the back wall

and the sugary brazen ones closer
under glass—blatantly beautiful loaves

kneaded, pressed, stroked, patted,
shaped by clever hands.

Outside on the bench curved like the curve
of his arm, in flickering sunlight

beneath the ginkgo tree, we watch
people come and go cradling warm loaves

close to their bodies, all anticipatory
inspiration, and we feed each other

apple croissants sprinkled
with cinnamon and sugar.

LUNCHEON ON THE GRASS

Oil on canvas, Edouard Manet

And didn't you know
it would end like this

in a glade by the river
your clothes puddled nearby

the outrage the scandal
your unrepentant gaze

like the river's constant glide
toward open water

Try to halt
the wheel of seasons

or a seed waiting in the desert
fifty years to bloom with rain

the rain all glint and silent touch
Think of the precarious dewdrop

clinging to a web
that catches morning light

You bring the river with you
beaded silver on your naked skin

drying in the open air

BIG DIPPER – *LA CASSEROLE*

After Alberto Rios

Never mind the bananas, pomegranates, avocados,
picked fresh from your poems,

or the rice spiced with chilies and cilantro, the soups
that simmer and steam; corn, fresh beans, and yellow
squash.

The ode to pie so temptingly coupled with desire
and you say, *I've just eaten too much.*

Your hunger feeds me, makes me hungry
for lightning and stars, light and love,

creosote after rain and orange-blossoms.
I've never lived in the desert, but I feel the heat.

GARDEN PRANKS

For Brian

Do you remember?
Sleeping beneath the night sky
declaring, with the confidence
of a three year old, *The moon is my friend.*

Morning visits to the garden
you loosened the grip of the bean tendrils,
spiraled the plants around their poles
in the opposite direction trying to convince
them, against the spin and pull of the earth,
they could choose their own way.

A robin's egg found on moss beneath the fir tree,
color of pure turquoise, a treasure you longed
to possess, but did not touch.

I wanted to give you the moon
so you would never feel alone.
I wanted you to know one almost
always has choices and that some things
are so precious you touch them
only with your heart
and a lifetime of memories.

YESTERDAY'S LIGHT

We keep coming back to what we gave up.
Lisel Mueller

So strong, this impulse,
to find the exact spot
near the swinging bridge
where the country store once stood.

The empty field owes me nothing.
I drive by slowly, follow
the river road and memories;
dark oiled floors, the fragrance
of blueberry buckle fresh
from the oven, a plump little woman,
housedress and apron, who stepped
from behind a curtained doorway,
scooped peach ice cream
on a summer day
sunlight muted through the maple.

This need to travel back
to find that depot of innocence.
The fifties steak house,
white and chrome and black;
its green awning long gone
the building now splashed
with garish red and yellow script
in a language I don't understand.
Near the heavy entrance door
I close my eyes, smell gardenia,
my prom date corsage,

picture the boy who pinned it on,
his eyes soft like brown velvet.

At the end of Main Street,
the fountain replaced
with a more efficient rotary,
stained glass windows
removed from the Spanish-style
church where, long ago,
friends gathered
to witness our wedding vows.

Now an arrow points
to the upper floor
and a neon sign flashes
in one of the clear window panes:
Tattoo Parlor—
the needle-prick of now,
the indelible imprint of then.

WHAT IF

What if the ultimate prize is that you choose
your happiest time and live in that state forever.

A moment when awareness of time passing
fades like a gingham quilt opened to sunlight;

a pattern of soft contentment, a patch of euphoria,
a blaze of orgasmic bliss, or just a quiet knowing.

Who would be with you
and would they feel the same?

Perhaps a greedy span of years
those bridging a life;

tender childhood days,
the sweet chocolate sensation of first love,

births and rebirths, and as you age,
falling in love with your life.

But then to release the sorrows
let them drift away like down from a thorny thistle.

Were the sorrows, are those sorrows,
necessary to your joy?

OBSERVATIONS OF AN OB/GYN NURSE

In memory of Dr. Tom Critchfield

The babies, CEOs of his life,
set the schedule, write the script.

They arrive in predawn hours
and the middle of the afternoon

unaware of an overflowing
waiting room or his need for a few

hours of uninterrupted sleep.
The police recognize his car,

escort him to the hospital
for those middle of the night calls.

Surgery, lunch in the hospital cafeteria,
then office hours where the babies,

bundled in mother's arms,
check in for a six-week visit

peaceful and slumbering, as if making up
for the sleep he missed.

At career's end, twin granddaughters
born on his birthday.

Memories streak across the mind's sky.
We need their bright, yet fleeting comfort.

His life of births, his solitary death.
This night Venus trembles

below the crescent moon
like a glistening tear.

SHE TURNED FIFTY

Have you ever noticed?
Barbie always walks
on tip-toes
mincing along
as if sneaking
up on Ken,
a flat-footed dude,
able to get
where he wants to go,
never mind what's
expected of him.
Only by wearing
spike heels
does she achieve
balance.
Hobbled,
as she is,
by her
acutely
angled shoes
she lacks
mobility
to run away
from
her not
so
perfect
life.

TILT

Sometimes I forget
how the earth spins and tilts,

shifts its tectonic plates
causing the ground to split

and groan and tremble.
How sun storms throw

radioactive darts in our direction
and burning boulders skim

the atmosphere. The rose window
high in the gable of our seaside

home records the sun's arc
and the moon's advances.

Its mullions split sunlight,
a shadowy web

that slips down the wall
its morning tracery spread across

the floor capturing the rhythm
and swirl of our staggering days.

On moonlit nights beams of light
pour through my window's

openings arranged in changing
curves and triangles, a rotation

I trust, forgetting I walk
on particles amassed around

a molten core, suspended
from nothing.

PART TWO

...as if what exists, exists
so that it can be lost
and become precious.
Lisel Mueller

FROM NAZIM HIKMET'S CELL

If I could see just one slice of sky
would it be enough?
to memorize the moods of clouds,
tally the shades of night into dawn.

Does light become more precious
as it angles through bars,
the geometric rightness
patterning the wall

and a single star, its cold burn
like a distant hope.

I would remember the unexplained
sweetness of a certain day
when winter turned toward spring.
Could one bear to think of plums,
lavender, mint...

Imprisoned, each mote suspended
in light becomes more than itself,
even this, a trace of earth,
a garden tilled into furrows
of the mind.

How Hikmet must have yearned
for silence, a bowl to hold
the comfort of his words.

I once was in wilderness beside
a lake. There was no sound,
no sound, a blue bowl of silence.

WHERE POEMS WINTER

I settle into a packed barrel of dreams.
Staves hold the gleaming apples in,

a hole near the bottom lets juice
run out. Here truth ferments:

a yellow barn rises, yes flies
above a sapphire lake,

an orchid, pressed between pages
of an ancient book, renewed by dew,

bees that touch and spin
words into a saffron cord,

a pen trapped and scribbling
in the corner of a blank page

like a swallow that enters an open
window, now desperate for sky.

ANNA'S HUMMINGBIRD

Response to *Instructions To Painters And Poets*
By Lawrence Ferlinghetti

Ferlinghetti asked painters and poets
how to paint sunlight on the face of life.
Their answers were ambiguous
as if guarding trade secrets.

How to mix the palette to paint
the choices of a life?
How to load our brushes with light?

In my garden, light arranges itself
among blossoms
in the coolness of morning,

arcs of violet, pink, blue, green;
bubbles of light
against a blur of wings

and there is no other word for it—
the tiny body, this iridescent jewel,

glimmers

a sudden shattering of color
as the bird paints sunlight
yes, unambiguously,
trading nothing.

THE SHAPE OF LONGING

In the round weight
of stone cupped within my hand
dense black and smooth
as a devil's eye

and there in the curve
of the gull's wing
as it angles into the bleak winter sky.

Its enigmatic silhouette
draws me to an improbable tryst—
a horizon that fades into night
or a sunrise that simmers beyond
mountains, concealing its source.

Why fill with the rumble of want
like a vagabond who bundles
his belongings, not knowing
where to go?

WELLINGTON TRAIN DISASTER

Stevens Pass, 1910

Snow falls fast as we drive
over the crest of the mountain,
head down the west side.

I cannot pass by this place
without thoughts of what happened
here one hundred years ago.

Feathery flakes whirligig
against the windshield, glitter
in the white beam of our headlights.

Most who travel this route don't know
how the sky threw thunderbolts
and lightning down the mountain

how the avalanche rampaged,
swept the trains into the gully, twisting
them into horrific abstract sculptures

how ninety-six people perished
after being stranded in the storm
four days, five nights.

Here evergreens spindle upward,
branches crusted white as if snow geese
had dropped their wings.

Yet the geese ascend sky's staircase
like angels scaling Jacob's ladder,
the earth falling away beneath them.

How to imagine such release.

TAMARACK

I travel east into the Cascades
to a small town my parents
came to as newlyweds,

follow double yellow lines,
the road too treacherous for passing,
search for a small cabin

where I was conceived. More gold
than yellow, the center lines
mimic the hue of autumn tamarack

released of its evergreen pretensions.
The tamaracks flare
above a scud of clouds

draped over the valley,
rise
toward snow-topped peaks.

Carried out of these mountains
curled like a leaf
in my mother's womb

I unfurled in a different place.
Return is like seeing the negative
from a long time ago,

a bright image that remains
for an instant
after you close your eyes.

EAST OF THE MOUNTAINS

For Fran

You know the disposition of grief
how it bends you like wheat,
an undulating field of waves,
swept by a searing wind.

How it twists what you know
to be true, not from lack
of kindness, but because
it knows no other way.

Grief comes disguised in blue
so intense it seems black,
but remember that tender time
in the spring, before summer's heat

dictates the landscape,
how morning dew lingers
in sheltered places and wild violets
flourish in the valley.

CASCADE SUITE

What overcomes him,
causes him to stop
at this particular place
west of Rainy Day Pass
near the Pacific Crest Trail?

Is it the resinous scent
coaxed from Grand fir and hemlock
by summer sun,

the jade river sliding
like ruched silk over a bed of stones,

the mists of waterfalls that spin
blue and violet prisms
above salal and Oregon grape,
asters and lupine, falling
like an amen on the skin?

Is it imagined echoes
poised to bounce from the granite
slabs and ravines of Liberty Bell
Mt. Fury and the Prophet

or mountain air
so pure there is no choice
but song.

I see him briefly as we flash
by in our car.

Pulled off to the side of the road
he perches on the tailgate of a truck,
French horn pressed against his lips,
tucked into his arms like a new bride.

WITHOUT NOTICE

Oak Harbor, Washington

Sometimes loss announces its intentions,
other times it arrives suddenly, without notice.

I learned Easter Sunday that it was gone—
the Garry Oak that had made peace with the sky

for three hundred thirty years. It once defined
the corner of my great-uncle's property,

a favorite uncle who was generous with kisses
and home-grown beefsteak tomatoes.

It had been felled early one morning, I was told,
by those who deemed it dangerous.

Loss creeps around the edges of helplessness
and we are like songbirds who have lost their

shelter and exuberant songs.

BEACON ROCK

Under a canopy of Oregon grape
a motionless rabbit. Its eyes
widen as I approach.

I know that swoop of fear,
how it swirls
out of nowhere

clutches me
midway up
the winding trail

to the pinnacle
of Beacon Rock,
this eight hundred fifty

foot monolith above
the Columbia River.
Yes, there's more to tell:

Did the unsuspecting wife sense
danger, balanced here on the core
of this ancient volcano?

Feel unease float around her
like dust motes
in sunlight?

The young wife
who mysteriously fell
to her death here

where silence sings
its sad song and clutches
the truth.

Alert at the edge of the cliff
I turn back, needing to touch
the solid face of basalt,

stroke its sun-warmed ribs.
Logic flies into the void
and above the river

a flock of silvery birds
turns all at once
flashing a dark underside.

BREATHE

Frightened, we hold
our breath, but that's not
what happened.

That summer day at the lake
so young, no reason
to think about consequences.

Sifting my mother's care
through my fingers was as easy
as breathing. Near the shore

a water slide. Ten steps up,
that irresistible curvy swish
to the bottom. I had asked again

and again. Been told, *No. Someday*
when you're a better swimmer,
yet I was drawn to that shiny

chute the way light glints
off a silver coin and strikes
the eye of a crow.

From the top of the slide,
a scaffold of independence,
I saw my mother resting

on the shore and quickly launched
myself down; such a perfect, forbidden
glide. In an instant I slipped

into the blue-green water
as smoothly as a button
through its loop

surprised I could not find
my footing. I watched shimmering
bubbles escape and rise,

curious observer of a strange, pale
light, a dreamy underwater world
where I floated, not knowing

I had slid off the edge
of all that was safe
and predictable.

FINDING OUR WAY

We talk about it now.
Who will go first.

We are like kids taking a dare
but there is no choice here.

How to loosen
the twining of two lives?

I will be comforted
in the home he built

how it encloses me
with the solid life we shaped.

I will hear the twang
and thump of hammer,

see his hands as I touch
the oil-rubbed finish of my desk.

He says he won't
be able to stay,

bear the sunlit rooms, the gardens
of sunflowers and lavender

golden beets and potatoes
that nourished us,

prepared in the kitchen
that overlooks the sea.

It's not sadness
just a curious reality

we have known all along
and somehow set aside

like an interesting chore
we will get back to

when the time is right.

FIFTY YEARS TOGETHER

There is something about saying goodnight
that feels like goodbye.

Pillows plumped, fingers entwined
like fretwork on a bridge we will cross

as we move in separate directions
into the silent villages of our dreams.

Moonlight will slant through the curtain
silver shards cast over our quiet bodies.

When I awake he will be gone.
We have folded the map of our sleep,

shaped it into another day.
I will find him in the garden,

droplets from the watering can
spilling him to the earth.

THE EVENING NEWS

She calls from across the country
feeling her way along the unfamiliar

corridors of widowhood. A right turn here,
lost at the next corner.

Sometimes it almost feels
as if he's here and I talk to him,

she says, things I need him to know.
You'll probably think I don't have enough

to do when I tell you this:
Every night I check out Brian Williams' ties.

Sometimes he wears the same tie
twice in one month.

Mostly stripes, mostly dark,
sometimes red or purple.

Tonight it's black and white.

BEACH ARCHITECTURE

In memory of Bob

Along the shore I see
imperfect and tilted shelters,
bleached driftwood stacked
into whimsical structures,
built with what's at hand.
No one believes
in their permanence.

We speak of his *passing*,
a fleeting word,
a sojourn where we live
in the shadow of parting.
How to shape our lives now
that the beam has fallen?
We will make what we can,
live within what we have built.

Now a turning tide
and at water's edge
a soggy heart
traced in the sand
wreathed
in beach pea blossoms.

SHADES OF NIGHT

Light stretches and yawns, but does not sleep,
covers itself in the borrowed blanket of night.

Awake, I gauge the mutations of light:
the darkness of deepest night an untouchable

softness that blots shapes onto the imagination
and below in the garden, pale narcissus glow,

sails on a dark sea. The night opens
the way jasmine is lured to bloom

in the shelter of darkness, a gradual release,
like an insight that has been there all along

measuring the shadows of time. Now dawn
escapes its opalescent shell; pastel tides move

across a naked daylight sky quietly
stalking the lingering ghost moon.

PART THREE

The seed is kicking
inside the earth.
Tomas Transtromer

THINGS I DIDN'T KNOW I LOVED

After Nazim Hikmet

So intent on sky, the fickle clouds,
the smack of salt, waves pushing
against the shore; the sun
begins its descent, spreads
its tail across Admiralty Inlet
like a mythical fish
weaving a sinuous path
toward the sea
and I love this light on water
and the earth too much...

Here a gull's feather
stuck upright in a mosaic
of rocks, these humble rocks
how they yield to the sea
their harmonies of lift and tumble,
syllables of rattle and release,
the weight and permanence
of what they say.
The agate carries the language
of upheaval, this translucent
vessel of glass
flung from volcanic fire.
How did I not know?
This love of stone.

BIOPSY

The first slice of day is best.
I choose the largest piece.

This last morning of summer
the perennial garden rain-faded,

the fields greening toward winter;
a road crew's chain saw cuts

the crust of silence clearing away
the willow that fell in a sudden

summer storm, an untimely
squall carrying more force

because it found us unaware,
changed the familiar landscape

in an instant to something
distant, unrecognizable.

How trusting we were that morning
as we raised the first cup of coffee

to our lips thinking everything
would remain the same.

WHAT WE REMEMBER

This morning, watching how the sun
slants through the slats of the arbor

infuses the air with the scent
of honeysuckle, I step into the yard

and find a four-point buck
not ten feet away.

He considers me intently
as I do him and I wonder...

I go back to the house, cut an apple
into slices and return.

He comes to me without hesitation
and, one by one, takes each slice

from my hand. Yes, I'm quite certain
this is the little buck I fed those years ago

when the antler buds had not yet
blossomed, here at this exact spot

in my garden; the little buck that nudged
my hand, impatient for more apple.

Now the imposing presence of that great
rack rising and dipping as he eats

his breath warm on my hand, the muscled
nearness of his wide chest and shoulders;

two creatures with a history
of trust and in his eyes an understanding

as quiet and sure as a guiding star.
I turn away as he takes the last slice.

NOT EXACTLY MANNA

We expect rain, driven by wind
that gives it a horizontal
zing, and dust, salt spray, thistles...

once in a while lightning,
like a saber hurling toward the bay
or a meteor shower that powders the night sky.

Fog comes quickly, drops
and tumbles through the evergreens,
slithers into the field's pockets

and after the meadow is freshly mown
what else could drop
from the fickle sky as crows
fly by carrying the remains of mice
in their greedy beaks.

They say an eagle once dropped
a salmon at Raymond Carver's feet
as he strolled along the shore.
"What the hell," he said.

Took it home, fried it in butter
and ate it.

THIS MOMENT OF GRACE

Alone on the street of a small town
I walk toward the light of a bakery

where young people work late
shaping stollen for Christmas tables

and the full moon hangs its silence
in my heart. The crisp winter night

arranges thoughts scattered like stars
into sharp focus, a perfect moment

that will ripen to memory.
Who can say what makes it so.

Like an authentic image captured
when the subject is unaware,

I see my life without smudges,
blurs, or margins and in that instant

I understand. I have always
felt well loved.

MOUNTAIN RETREAT

Outside my window a tamarack
in the dim light of October.

Well into its transformation,
golden needles cluster around the trunk,

radiate out to the still green
tips of the branches.

Nature's renovation, this deciduous conifer,
for much of the year masquerading

as an evergreen, now a bright flame
in the midst of the forest.

We should not be surprised.
Patterns replicate in all of us

as we show each other who we are.
Why then are we so often startled

by what seems like sudden change—
how reality stripped of its pretenses

appears as something else.

THE HUNTER

You point toward Orion
and I find the white burn
of three stars like wise men
traveling toward truth

and here I am fingering my way
along corridors of night,
intersections without signs,
entrance or exit not clearly marked

a seeker without a sword
learning to gauge stars.
I find them in spindrift
and sand, orb webs and dew.

They are everywhere
and yes, different.
The golden flicker of quaking
aspen in rarified autumn air,

constellations in a skiff
of thistledown and mica's dust;
a blink of silver or blue
on a sheer face of granite.

And what of winter's crystals,
prisms of transient light
spinning in Orion's chill.

I know of the massive red star
nearing the end of its life
within the hunter's range

an explosion that will pierce
what we know of light, scatter
the tears of seven lost sisters
into the night.

WINTER STILLNESS

Crockett Prairie, Whidbey Island

Light from the window angles
across the snow-laden field,
soundless flakes building
upon themselves
like small-parceled
courage.

The snow glows, covers rabbit hole,
the runs of vole as dusk deepens,
edges into the forest, a dark sweep
of purple that silences bird call,
and the skittering of small,
brave creatures.

Venus billows from the bell
of the moon, icy light riveting
darkness, striking the willow,
wild rose thicket, and evergreen
boughs now fatigued
with snow.

It's what I do not hear
that makes me listen, the space
between words breathing
what is unspeakable, the pause
between heartbeats that still
has rhythm.

THE WOMEN WHO LOVED HIM

His bride rests on the top step
of the porch, his boyhood home,
where he sat in the cool of evening
scratching Pete's ears
and now the dog looks down
the dusty road where the two of them
had walked; the young Marine,
his old dog.

His mother sits inside by the window,
remembers the way he paused,
gazed out over the fields
always in the same place
before moving into the shadow
of the Garry Oak.

Does it matter which war?
War is war, some say.
Loss is loss, carried home
in silence, assembled in the grit
and creases of combat boots.

After the funeral, I heard
the lieutenant say,
when he reached out to present
the dog tags to Paul's wife,
Paul's mother held out her hand.

ALMANAC

My grandparents owned the land,
worked the land, bound
to the earth by seasons of planting
and harvest.

They watched the sky, the habits
of birds, hues of sunset,
the moods of moon and clouds,
the disposition of air.
They inhaled the coming season,
let it brighten their blood
for the work ahead.

Soil sifted through their fingers
imbedded beneath their nails
and this is what they knew;
this rhythm circling the years.
They never left their land;
each in their own time
settled deeper.

PNEUMA

In memory of Ryan
November 4, 1986 – July 3, 2010

The day of Pentecost the wind
and Spirit came together.

A powerful wind.
A vital Spirit.

So close you couldn't tell
one from the other

the way the sea and sky
meet at the horizon, become one.

This young man, living so close to breath,
created more space for Spirit.

The courage he pulled
from molecules of air

did not rage through the limbs
of the Garry Oak

nor howl in the vestry
of his life.

Hear the bell in the church tower
how it displaces summer's stillness.

Feel the sigh of breeze
upon your cheek,

the sudden shifting currents
that rumple your hair,

how it loosens the oak leaf that falls
lightly on your shoulder.

SANDY HOOK WINTER

"To bear witness to the death, without
being broken by the weight of it"
M.L. Stedman, The Light Between Oceans

An empty bench beneath
an ice-encrusted tree. I walk
through snow to reach this quiet place

and sit facing a dim forest shadowed
in mist, needing the false comfort
of a partial view.

Shapes that lay claim to bareness.
Time suspended in tiny
crystals that cover everything.

No one can make sense of it.
The landscape, of what we thought
to be true, changed forever.

A chill glazes the crevices
of the inner life; a colorless rime
that seals our grief.

Perhaps sorrow will find
its way to rest
in stillness.

I turn. Behind me a branch
uncleanly broken, held
by one fibrous strand.

COUNTERPOINT

Dreams twist into the night,
one strand moves away
the other coils back.

I wander through fields, a forest
of cedar and fir, ride escalators
into the skeletal reaches

of department stores, medical centers.
Carry lost children across rivers of ice,
pledge their safe return.

Ascend through multistoried homes:
an ivy covered mansion, a tree house,
the tubular home where architects gather.

Walk into the city, a Paris hotel,
loop and retrace my path, always
searching for a way to return.

What I long to return to is not clear.
I circle the mystery of my dreams
like volcanic ash that continues

to orbit the earth
scattering bits and pieces
of itself here and there.

WHEN SILENCE WAS ENOUGH

For my father

Not the sort of silence that falls with snow,
nor the interlude between heartbeats;

more the musical pattering of raindrops—
the things we say to each other

barely penetrating the surface. Questions unasked
leave a mineralized vein of history

and more than that, nuggets of a life unclaimed
on a stream bed of everyday conversation.

Evenings, returning from work, he splashed
the tiredness from his face, water going beyond

where it was expected, a fountain of exuberance,
and we held out our hands to catch the drops.

The happy child, the competent father—
feelings you know to be true only half

the bond. Now questions...
The questions...

What did you dream and what got away?

GREEN '58 CHEVY APACHE TRUCK

The only time I saw my father cry
was when our dog died.

The call came early Sunday morning
heart too weak to withstand surgery.

Mac, our boxer, runt of the litter,
grew tall and stately, chest blazed

in white. He loved to ride
in the passenger seat of my father's

pickup like two teenagers
on a first date. They were a familiar pair,

joyriding around our small town,
Mac nudging ever closer

until he could lean against my father,
both of them behind the wheel.

After my father put down the phone
that morning he said he needed

to be gone for a while.
Drove away in the truck.

A PARTING GIFT

Lillian Hanson Putnam, 1889 – 1958

Found in a box of old photos a silver hand mirror,
her monogram engraved on the back

surrounded by a wreath of ribbons and leaves.
A small dent, the beveled glass cracked

into two uneven parts. Age sixteen, she traveled
from Michigan to the Pacific Northwest,

never to see her family again
until she returned forty years later.

The etching on the handle worn smooth,
the mirror is heavy in my hand

as I remember the cold mornings she warmed
my clothes by the woodstove before helping me dress,

how on visits I slept with her because *a child*
could become frightened alone in a dark room.

Does one ever understand love when it is ever present?
We gathered trilliums, hunted for morel mushrooms,

picked blackberries, waded in the creek
and watched pollywogs sprout legs.

Now she sleeps under the eaves of my musings
and in the mists that refresh my life.

PART FOUR

A moment is a moment and
that moment is everything.
Alberto Rios

CURRICULUM VITAE

After Lisel Mueller

The day I was born my parents labored:
My mother for obvious reasons,
my father to expel a kidney stone.

Gloom of the Great Depression behind them
the glare of war in their eyes
my parents gave me a hero's welcome.

Quiet times on the farm. Buttercups,
bleeding hearts, barn cats, lady bugs,
learning to cope with a happy childhood.

Afternoons reading in the moss-covered
junction of a huge maple tree
I found the shelter and bliss of words.

A hospital was my classroom:
The cosmic echo of a newborn's first cry,
the unbroken silence of the departed.

A deep, quixotic voice led me to an altar
of promises, nights of burning stars, the two-part
invention of sons, a breathless rush of years.

Stacking lumber to build a home, nails buried deep
in safety, contentment. Ordinary moments
that sparked and glowed.

Then loss and more loss. Lost in a dark forest
of grief. Compassion held out its hand
and I hung on.

The hurt of beauty, an indefinable longing,
recommended me to poetry. Steady work,
polishing the cells of the hive

to receive the sweetness.

THE HONEYCOMB CONJECTURE

A honey bee brushed my lips,
a soft tap, as if something necessary
would emerge.

How to shape six-sided words
that fit precisely, a space to inhabit,
polished cells spilling

an elixir of light,
syllables suspended in amber,
a lexis of industry and purpose.

I like to think of those meticulous chambers
burnished with an ageless patina
and the pollen-dusted bee

attentive within the penstemon's bell,
a golden tongue chiming,
all is new, an exquisite language

of communion.

HOMAGE TO PLATT ROGERS SPENCER

It mattered then, strokes
as elegant as butterfly wings.
Loops and scrolls inked
on pages of yearbooks,
birth certificates, bank contracts
and everyday posts—envelopes,
recipe cards, and twining
down grocery lists.

It twirled away at the end
of a signature, returning to underline
the given and inherited, a definition
of lightness born more of respect
than vanity.

We sat at little oak desks, hooked
to each other like railroad cars
and practiced the Palmer Method,
loops perfectly coiled
as though they might spring
off the page.

Now time is our master.
Calls, emails, texts sliding off
the tip of a swirling whip,
all shockingly similar missives
that strike with a staccato beat.

Down by the road the old-fashioned
mailbox waits. Amid a flurry

of bills and ads, occasionally
a hand written letter. Opening
the letter's envelope is like slipping
between sheets dried in an island breeze.

Further down the road an islander
has painted her mailbox tea rose pink.
On the side, in lovely Spencerian
script, her simple directive:
Love Letters Only.

DUENDE

So little separates us from the sea.
High tide churned by wind,

the shingle consumed by swells
that break on shore, spume

rising; briny geysers explode,
splinter in the moonlight,

electrical charges trill
our brain cells with irrational

daring. Now the waves outshout us.
Evan runs to see how close

he can get before being overtaken.
I hold my breath until he turns,

races toward safety, the sea
breathing hard against his back.

Come to me. Come to me
my not quite full-grown boy.

DOING DISHES

She said she had always wanted to do it;
throw away dirty dishes rather than wash them

and she did, after breakfast, toss the blue, green,
orange, and yellow Fiestaware into the trash.

Transferring from New York to Germany
with her husband and children,

the movers coming that day, she chucked the dishes
in among the banana peels, egg shells, coffee grounds,

bits of bacon, paper towels and called it good.
What she could not know is that a young mother

in that very town received a much needed set
of tableware when her husband returned

home from work that evening. Bright dishes
that showed up chipped and grubby

like old friends with egg on their faces.

COOKIE BAKERS

It’s not the memory of the 1940’s kitchen,
radio tuned to Queen for a Day,

or the Betty Crocker Cookbook splayed
beside the Sunbeam mixer.

Not even the fragrance of snickerdoodles,
hot from the oven, that summons

me, the child, yearning to lay my head,
one more time, on my mother’s lap.

It’s a husk of oatmeal that I find
between the pages of her cookbook

long after she’s gone.

CHOICES WE MAKE WHEN WE ARE TOO YOUNG TO MAKE THEM

Evenings at the table with my father,
stewing over algebraic equations,

chemical reactions, my young life
sloped toward science and healing.

He didn't recognize, nor did I,
how I fingered letters

the way the devout touch
prayer beads, that I held them

up to my ear to hear the music
they made when strung together,

a child rearranging alphabet blocks,
balancing them into a fragile

tower that spelled out something
I was too young to understand.

I can't say how we know
we please, without hearing the exact

words, but I knew. His pride in me
slipped into my hands with soup spoons

and Yardley's soap as I fed and bathed him
during the last months of his life.

I often wonder if he is surprised,
living as he does, in the spaces

between words, there among
the pages of my books.

A MOTHER REMEMBERS

Never mind that they are three successful
men living, by chance, in the same city,
complete with wives and children.

I see ten year olds: my son, his two boyhood
companions who ate batch after batch
of Swedish pancakes in my kitchen,

carried out clandestine adventure
under cover of weeds in a nearby field.
I questioned their pallor, heard confessions,

held their heads as they rid themselves
of Redman Chewing Tobacco.
Neighborhood dogs romped with the boys,

used the vacant lot as a repository
of all that is natural, where the boys
played football; those end runs

and slides, those gag-inducing maneuvers.
Yes, we discuss these memories
over dinner while their little ones

listen to the tales of these strange men
who are their fathers.

MOTHER'S DAY

My oldest son is the one
who keeps me guessing.

A neon-pink sticker placed
on my rear bumper that I didn't

notice for a week, then discovered
in the K-Mart parking lot:

Follow me
to the flashing blue light special.

The one who hid our television
in a back closet making me think

we had been burglarized
and who, as a creative teen,

surreptitiously hung an artful banner
on the side wall of the local bank

which read: *On Sale, One Dollar Bills*
Seventy Five Cents.

Standing back to admire his inspired
endeavor he realized the bank

was directly across the street from
the town's police department.

So it is no surprise that he gave me
a gift for Mother's Day

which I'm fairly sure
not many other mothers received.

An elegant cobra-like houseplant
that catches flies, its webbed hood

suspended over an open mouth
that whispers, *I'm hungry,*

I'm hungry.

GRANDDAUGHTER

She came to us when least expected,
a baby girl in the midst of boy cousins,
uncles and a brother twelve years her senior.

Now five, just a slip of a thing,
she lives big. When asked
where she would like to go

for a family vacation she says,
Somewhere fancy, then adds
Paris, France.

She loves arranging flowers
so the *inside, quiet colors*
go with the loud ones,

ballet, books, baking biscuits,
concerts with her father
and shopping for antiques.

She presses against the window
each night before climbing into bed
and first thing in the morning

as if to catch the glitter of the world.
At the end of her visit I will wash
the windows, make sure to wipe around,

not over, those tiny nose and hand prints.
This morning Grandpa asks her
 how she likes her toast and she says,

Toast it until the smoke alarm goes off.

THE LESSON OF PLUMS

After year-long illness, a dream.
My doctor stands in the center
of a cultivated field,
the furrows deep and straight.
His brown suit blends
with the richness of the dark soil.
Arms extended, palms open,
his words travel through
sunlit air: *You are ready to grow.*

So simple, so hackneyed,
yet when I awake I know it's over,
the illness that blew in
like a menacing wind and me
a trembling leaf clinging
to what I knew of strength—
now nearly floating
in an autonomy of lightness.

Sometimes it's not about
seeking, but of receiving,
the way a plum takes in light,
an inner ripening that cracks
its perfect purple skin,
and sweetness, an amber rivulet,
crusts along the gash.

COUNTRY WOMAN

I look for answers everywhere now.
When I was young I didn't know
the questions.

I notice how gulls follow
the tractor as it turns the earth,
how they know where to go
to be nourished,

the dark furrows
of the newly plowed field
so like years folding
upon themselves,
what was there buried
by the slice of change.

Cloud-shadows move
across the prairie,
transient darkness
that compliments the light

and it may be all about light,
yet perhaps we cannot bear
the invariable
intensity of illumination.

I think about the glitter
of my young self
and know the girl breathes
beyond memory...

GYROSCOPE

With thanks to Bob Schieffer

The hardest questions are the ones the children ask,
the ones we tuck away to think about later

or never. Their questions, like poppies that push
through cracks in the sidewalk, lift tender stems

to sunlight, bloom against all odds. The young
need to know and how are we to answer?

Why the bad man shot the kids, why the mountain
came apart, covered all those people.

Why rogue waves climb the shore, predator birds
dive, carry away small animals.

These questions, like embers in my mouth;
singed words, charred reason.

Today, summer balances like a gyroscope
on spring's cord. A doe rests in the shade

of the lilac. Three hummingbirds play
their improvisational gig among the coral bells,

the fields high on sweet smelling hay,
and I search, like a feral cat that roams

the countryside, trying to find food
to nourish the young.

TESTIMONY OF RAIN

The storm rants through the Strait
of Juan de Fuca, many voices
threatening, yet exhilarating,
this dark night, as it sweeps
breakers onshore, batters
the stand of twisted evergreens.
How to distinguish where one sound
ends, another begins; a mash
of sky and sea, the thrashing
arms of trees.

The storm unravels its ball of fury
and moves on. Now the syncopated
dance of raindrops on the cabin
roof, a voice that repeats a familiar
childhood story. When did my young
life end this one begin?

I remember one moment, my son
home from college, us walking
together in soft rain. He puts his arm
around me, pulls me into a deep puddle.
Holding hands we jump up and down
splashing like demented toddlers.

SUMMER FOG

Fog swirls over the hill and settles
on Admiralty Inlet like a fresh
comforter shaken over a restful bed.

I hear the ferry's heartbeat
then see its dim shape
ghost into the harbor.

A heron glides through the mist
hitching a ride on floating
driftwood the way a munificent spirit
may encircle an unsuspecting soul.

As I leave the shore and walk
into the forest, cedar-scented clouds
of fog obscure the path. I imagine
those creatures that live so deep
in the sea's darkness
they lose their need for eyes.

Isolated now in dense fog,
the need to see what lies beyond,
yet the delicious mystery
of not knowing.

SUBMERGED

A flotilla of mergansers floats by on an outgoing tide
their reflections splayed on the blue-green water.
They duck below the surface of the bay, disappear,
pop up nibbling on small fish.

How would it feel to disappear, if only for a moment,
dip below the surface of a life, go deep
to find what truly nourishes
and if we were to look back at the reflection
left in the world, would it be beautiful?

ABOUT THE AUTHOR

Lois Parker Edstrom, a retired nurse, began writing poetry ten years ago. Her poems have appeared in literary journals such as *Borderlands: Texas Poetry Review*, *Birmingham Arts Journal*, *Clackamas Literary Review*, *Floating Bridge Review*, *Rock & Sling*, *Connecticut River Review*, *Adanna*, and *Mobius*. Her chapbook, *What Brings Us To Water* won the Poetica Publishing Chapbook Award, 2010 and a second collection, *What's To Be Done With Beauty*, was published by Creative Justice Press, 2012.

She received two Hackney National Literary Awards, Outrider Press Grand Prize, and the Westmoreland Award, among others. Her poetry has been adapted to dance and performed by the Bellingham Repertory Dance Company.

A native of the Pacific Northwest, she lives off the coast of Washington, on Whidbey Island, with her husband and resident deer, rabbits, owls, and herons. The beauty of the island and her love of art inspire much of her work.

CPSIA information can be obtained
at www.ICGtesting.com
Printed in the USA
FFOW03n0543290318
46102091-47132FF